CARBON BLOCK PUZZLE

Sirish Subash

CARBON BLOCK PUZZLE© 2021 Sirish Subash
All rights reserved. This book is protected under the copyright laws of the United States of America. This book may not be copied or reprinted for commercial gain or profit.

For worldwide distribution
ISBN: 978-0-578-82923-4
LCCN: 2021902607

CARBON BLOCK PUZZLE

*"We are the first generation to be able to **end poverty**, and the last generation that can take steps to avoid the worst impacts of **climate change**.*

*Future generations will judge us harshly if we fail to uphold our **moral and historical** responsibilities."*

- BAN KI-MOON

****

*"No challenge poses a greater threat to future generations than **climate change**."*

- BARACK OBAMA

CONTENTS

FOREWORD		1
AUTHOR'S NOTE		3
INTRODUCTION		5
1.	WHAT IS CARBON BLOCK PUZZLE?	6
2.	ARE WE REALLY PLAYING IT?	10
3.	PLACING THE BLOCKS	15
4.	MEGA BLOCKS	21
5.	DESTROY THE BLOCKS	27
6.	GAME OVER	32
7.	ONE FOR ALL	37
8.	LEVEL UP	41
9.	WINNING THE GAME	48
10.	LOOK WHO IS PLAYING	61
11.	IN IT TO WIN IT	68
MASTER THE GAME: MORE INFORMATION		71
AFTERWORD		76
GLOSSARY		79
REFERENCES		86

FOREWORD

I first met Sirish when he entered kindergarten. His teacher shared a piece of Sirish's writing with me, in which he had drawn a picture of a happy family playing outside, observing a rainbow. Each arc of the rainbow was drawn showing the varying wavelengths of each band of light. When I asked Sirish to tell me about his drawing, he began to explain the relationship of each wavelength to the color of light we saw and explained to me that there was such a thing as the "electromagnetic spectrum." He was 6 years old.

Since then, I have watched Sirish grow as an avid observer of the world around him. He has a deep desire to investigate and understand the phenomenon he sees. But this is not enough for Sirish, he has the goal of sharing what he has learned with others and make a difference in the world.

Carbon Block Puzzle is Sirish's first book, and he aims to do just that…make a difference in people's lives. Sirish uses the game of Block Puzzle and its puzzle pieces, or blocks, as a model for climate change. He gives us an explanation of causes as well as a plan for "winning the game."

As I read through *Carbon Block Puzzle,* I was struck by how clearly I could hear Sirish's voice. I could hear him talking to me about his most recent discovery…that same young man who told me so earnestly about the visible light spectrum at the beginning of his school experience. I look forward to hearing more of Sirish's future investigations.

Carpe Diem!

Angela Herbel,

Gifted Educator.

AUTHOR'S NOTE

My journey to writing Carbon Block Puzzle started when I watched the documentary *Before the Flood* at age six. While watching it, my heart broke. I felt terribly sad for people who are suffering to get even their essential needs due to climate change. Even though I was sad, I still wanted to help stop climate change. I didn't want those people to suffer much more. It was deeply upsetting, but it was also a strong driving force to prevent climate change. So, I then decided to dive deeper into it.

From then on, I frequently came up with ways to prevent climate change. Fast forward to 2019, and I gave a speech about climate change to my family, friends, and neighbors. Some of them said that they were influenced by my speech and were helping stop climate change at their house. I realized that my words could influence people and getting them to a larger audience could cause a noticeable change. I decided I would make a comprehensive and easy-to-understand book on climate change. The reason this is so important that climate change is threatening humanity now. If people don't act, and speak up now, then humanity and everything we cherish will cease to exist.

"I read a book one day and my whole life was changed."

– Orhan Pamuk

Carbon Block Puzzle is a straightforward and compendious way to learn the basics of climate change.

Climate change is a critical issue nowadays and it's hard to tell right from wrong.

The effects of climate change are already happening. The first inklings of damage have already been done. Unless more people learn about climate change, the darkest days of climate change could come soon. That's where Carbon Block Puzzle comes in. It educates readers on climate change and how to prevent it. Only if truth prevails will the right thing happen, and only then will humanity be safe from climate change.

This book not only educates people but encourages them to do the right thing and help stop climate change, and to borrow Bill Nye's words, "dare I say it, save the world !"

Not only that, but Carbon Block Puzzle does this in a fun way, using the video game Block Puzzle. Above all, "a book is a foundation for education," and that's exactly what we need right now.

Sirish Subash

INTRODUCTION

WHAT IF I told you that the world is almost at game over in a life or death game of Block Puzzle? You'd probably say, "YOU ARE CRAZY!", and walk away, but it's true! We are at a now or never time in this game of Block Puzzle.

How do we play this game anyway? That's one of the things you're going to learn in this book. But what is this game of Block Puzzle? It's called **CLIMATE CHANGE**. What is climate change? In a nutshell, climate change is the manmade warming of Earth caused by **greenhouse gases**.

This game of Block Puzzle isn't any game of Block Puzzle. This is Carbon Block Puzzle, where the blocks are greenhouse gases. Whether you know it or not, we are all part of this game of Block Puzzle and we are all placing the blocks.

1. WHAT IS CARBON BLOCK PUZZLE?

CARBON BLOCK PUZZLE IS the large-scale version of Block Puzzle which earth is playing right now. It works like any game of Block Puzzle. There are one by one blocks of **carbon dioxide**. There are also larger blocks of super pollutants. Collectively, these blocks are classified as greenhouse gases. Greenhouse gases cause the greenhouse effect. As the name says, the greenhouse effect works just like a greenhouse. A greenhouse is a shelter usually made of glass used for growing plants.

Greenhouse gases act like glass by trapping in heat. This creates changes in climate and weather patterns. This is the driving force behind Carbon Block Puzzle.

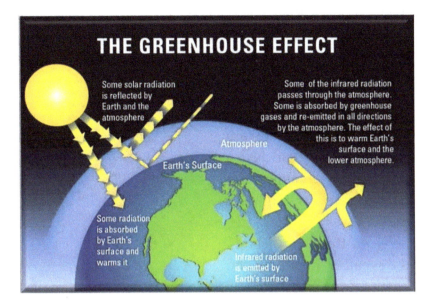

Credit: https://royalsociety.org/
Greenhouse gases in the atmosphere, including water vapor, carbon dioxide, methane, and nitrous oxide, absorb heat energy and emit it in all directions (including downwards), keeping Earth's surface and lower atmosphere warm. Adding more greenhouse gases to the atmosphere enhances the effect, making Earth's surface and lower atmosphere even warmer. Image based on a figure from US EPA.

WHAT ARE CLIMATE AND WEATHER?

You wake up in the morning and check the weather channel. What you see flashing across your screen is an often misunderstood topic. Weather is the current meteorological condition of an area. Weather changes every day.

You might say, "I thought weather and climate are the same." If so, you're wrong. Climate and weather are entirely different things. Climate changes over a long period of time. In fact, a literal definition of climate is weather over a long period of time. Usually, climate is an average of weather over 30 years. Climate can be derived from weather patterns. One thing about climate is that it's the most straightforward proof of climate change you can see now.

The differences between weather and climate are more intricate than just a time scale. The table in the next page shows some of the other differences between the two. Overall, the weather is mostly the result of the meteorological elements and the climate is mostly a summary of them.

> **DID YOU KNOW?**
>
> One billion tonnes of water fall every minute around the Earth!

Credit: Berkeley Earth - Global Average Temperature Anomaly

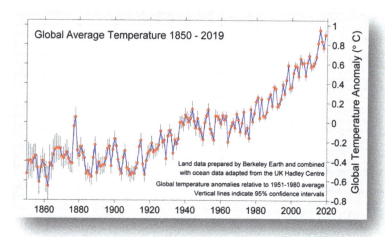

WEATHER	CLIMATE
Short term state of the atmosphere	Long term pattern of the weather
Weather can be defined as the atmosphere at a given time and place, with respect to variables such as wind, moisture, storms, snow, temperature, barometric pressure.	Climate is defined as the various atmospheric conditions which include rainfall, humidity, and other meteorological elements in a region over a long period.
Weather conditions may vary at intervals of a few hours or of a few days	Climate does not change as frequently
Can vary from time to time or location to location.	Average weather over many years in one specific place.
Example: Nor' Easter, Hurricane, Heat Wave, etc.,	Example: Average high and low temperatures

2. ARE WE REALLY PLAYING IT?

YES, WE ARE! Some people don't believe in climate change simply because it's horrifying! If someone said that the world is about to end, you probably wouldn't believe them, right? This is the same case with climate change non-believers. In fact, we are headed for that! This is one major reason that some people don't believe in climate change. It's only logical explanation is that you wouldn't believe something so dramatic and alarming! Some people who disbelieve in climate change usually point out the fact that we lack evidence and proof that climate change exists. The lack of proof is because we only have data reaching so far back and climate change just started accelerating to a noticeable scale (now it's accelerating exponentially).

Global warming skeptics say that the placement of weather stations in urban areas increases the temperature measurements due to the buildings reflecting and concentrating the heat. This can easily be opposed since most temperature measurements are taken far away from big cities.

> **NOT-SO-FUN-FACT**
>
> Severe weather causes billions of dollars in damage.

Some other climate skeptics say that the temperature where they live fluctuates frequently and often cools. This is wrong. Global warming is, well <u>GLOBAL</u>. The temperature is taken as an average of temperature all over the globe. When you look at the global temperature results, it is rising.

Climate change is real on the grounds that the global temperature has increased by 0.85° Celsius. The earth is supposed to be cooling due to the earth's orbit going farther away from the sun because of **Milankovitch cycles**. People all around the world are suffering due to many effects of climate change such as extreme weather, **malnutrition**, warming oceans, melting ice sheets, sea-level rise, **ocean acidification**.

One large example is the Australian bushfires. The bushfires are large enough to create their own climate! These bushfires are caused by extreme heat and a dry environment.

Carbon Block Puzzle

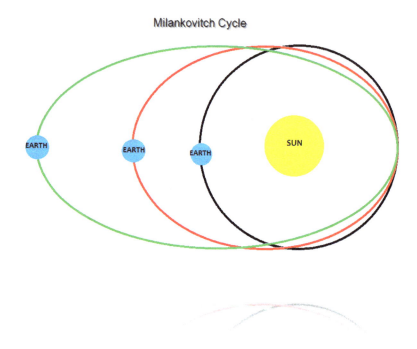

Milankovitch cycles are caused by Earth's orbit becoming more or less elliptical over time. The change in how elliptical Earth's orbit is affects how close to the sun it is, which in turn affects the climate.

Another effect of this heat is bodies of water drying up, such as Lake Chad in Africa, shown in the pictures below. Lake Chad was the fourth largest in Africa in the 1960s, at more than 2600 km². As of 2020, it's 1540 km². As you can see, it's drastically shrunk, not only as an effect of this heat but also owing to overuse. These are some of many of the effects of the blocks in Carbon Block Puzzles piling up. **We really are playing Carbon Block Puzzle!**

Lake Chad, Africa - 1973
Credit: earthobservatory.nasa.gov

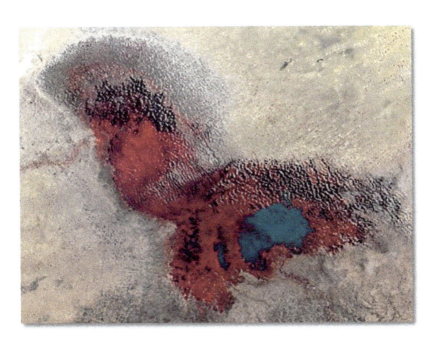

Lake Chad, Africa - 2017
Credit: earthobservatory.nasa.gov

Sea Level Rise – Kiribati

Credit: Maarten van Aalst/ World Bank
Rising sea levels and ocean temperatures caused by global warming threaten the people, economy, and very existence of Kiribati, a low-lying island nation composed of coral atolls in the tropical Pacific

3. PLACING THE BLOCKS

FIRST LET'S INTRODUCE ourselves to the most common block in Carbon Block Puzzle, carbon dioxide (CO_2). Watch out! Though CO_2 has a very small capability to trap heat, there is a lot of it. It is a major component of the carbon cycle.

CO_2 is one of the greenhouse gases. It is made up of two **elements.** Carbon and oxygen (which make CO_2) are everywhere.

DID YOU KNOW?

The origin of the word carbon comes from the word *"carbo"* which is Latin for coal. Roughly 99% of carbon is stored deep within the earth's surface.

Carbon Block Puzzle

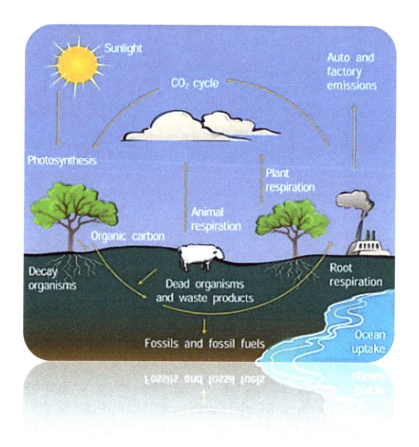

Credit: UCAR
A simple diagram of the parts of the carbon cycle, emphasizing the terrestrial (land-based) parts of the cycle.

CARBON CYCLE

The carbon cycle recycles carbon atoms. Carbon is the basis of every living thing in the world. The reason this is important when it comes to climate change is that the carbon is usually in the form of CO_2. In the carbon cycle, animals take in oxygen and release CO_2. Plants absorb CO_2 and emit oxygen. Plants also respire. That's when they release CO_2. Currently the plants' respiration rates are less than their CO_2 intake rates. As temperatures rise their respiration rates increase. This keeps a balance – a very delicate balance.

When plants and animals die, they release some CO_2 into the atmosphere. The rest of the CO_2 that will be locked away inside the body is consumed by **decomposers** and/or becomes fossil fuel. Even so, some carbon is locked away in the form of minerals.

FOSSIL FUELS

Fossil fuels are a type of non-renewable energy that comes from ancient **organic matter** from the **Carboniferous period**. There are three main fossil fuels: oil, which comes from tiny creatures that lived under the sea which got exposed to high pressure; coal, which comes from plant material that got exposed to high pressure and heat; and natural gas formed in the same way as oil, except there was more heat and pressure. Fossil fuels used to stay in the ground. Now people are extracting fossil fuels from underground and burning them, releasing CO_2.

Fossil fuels are commonly used because they have a high energy density. Fossil fuels have a major flaw: their energy is extracted in a way that only retrieves 30 % of the energy stored away in them. Fossil fuels have powered the way to industrialization, which started to stray away from nature's delicate balance, tipping it a bit. And with industrialization came climate change. In the chart below, you can see the major sources of greenhouse gases in the US. Agriculture is the smallest source at 9%. Commercial and residential sources rank next at 12%. The other three account for 79% percent of all greenhouse gas emissions. In third is industry at 22%. Next up is electricity, at 28%. The largest source of all is transportation, at 29%. If you look closely you'll see that the more a sector strays from nature's balance, the more greenhouse gases it emits. Fossil fuels are a major cause of climate change, and transportation plays a key part in them.

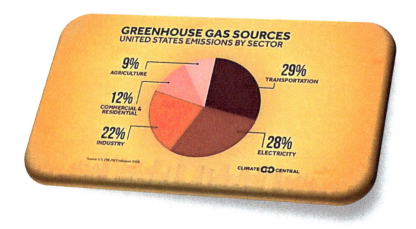

Credit: Climatecentral.org
GHG Sources US - Emissions by Sector - 2020

TRANSPORTATION

Practically all forms of transportation use fossil fuels. In fact, planes (on the short-haul) emit 175 grams of CO_2/km per person. They use most of it to get airborne. The average car emits 100 grams of CO_2/km per person. Cars emit 41% of all CO_2 emissions due to transportation! If you would rather take a bus, you would be emitting 75 grams of CO_2/km per passenger. Lastly, we have trains that emit 50 grams of CO_2/km per passenger.

Transportation emits 14% of all greenhouse gases (worldwide). As you can see, cars are one of the biggest criminals behind climate change.

DOES MY FOOD HARM THE EARTH?

> **NOT-SO-FUN-FACT**
>
> Humanity adds about 5.5 billion tons of CO_2 into the atmosphere each year, most of which goes into it directly.

Yes! This is mind-bending because our food comes from plants and animals, that were cycling CO_2 through the atmosphere and into their bodies. This keeps too much CO_2 from accumulating into the air (as mentioned earlier in this chapter). But why does our food harm the earth? Here are the largest ways that food contributes to climate change. When farms are built, large swaths of forest get cleared to make room for farmland. This releases huge amounts of CO_2 stored in trees while eliminating **carbon sinks** (something that absorbs more CO_2 than it releases). Fossil fuels are used in operating farm machines, making fertilizer, shipping foods, packaging, and processing. When cows, goats, and sheep digest their food, they release methane, which is a very potent greenhouse gas. Animal manure and rice paddies also release methane. We will be talking more about methane in the next chapter. Fertilizers also release nitrous oxide, which is another greenhouse gas 300 times more potent than CO_2. Growing livestock takes part in 70% of all agricultural land use, which is 30% of all the earth's land. Livestock releases 18% of all greenhouse gases such as methane and nitrous oxide. This means what you eat can change the world!

We've caught the culprit red-handed! But wait, there are other types of blocks too!

4. MEGA BLOCKS

SOME OF THE nastier culprits fall into this category: **super pollutants**. The most well-known mega block is methane. Let's get a good grip on just how nasty it is. It is 24 times stronger than CO_2 (according to the Environmental Defense Fund). There is less methane put into the air than CO_2, but it still plays a key role in climate change.

Credit: US Environmental Protection Agency

TABLE 1
Global warming potential, lifetime, and primary source of super pollutants

Super Pollutant	Global warming potential (100-year)	Lifetime in atmosphere	Primary source
Methane	21	12 years	Agriculture, mobile sources, electricity generation
Black carbon, or soot	330-2,240	Days to weeks	Incomplete combustion of fossil fuels, biofuels, biomass
Hydrofluorocarbons, or HFCs	140-11,700	15 years on average	Substitution of ODS, electricity generation

Source: U.S. Environmental Protection Agency.

Super Pollutants – Global warming potential (The number of times more powerful than CO_2 a greenhouse gas is), Lifetime in the atmosphere, and Primary Sources.

METHANE (CH_4)

Methane has an impact on climate change, second only to that of CO_2. In fact, it can impact the number of other greenhouse gases in the atmosphere. Methane comes from many sources, and the largest are the oil and gas industries.

Over the course of two decades, methane is eighty-four times more powerful than CO_2. Methane's lifetime in the atmosphere is twelve years. For every molecule of methane released in the atmosphere by natural sources, two are released by human beings, meaning the amount of methane released into the atmosphere has tripled.

> **DID YOU KNOW?**
>
> Another name for methane is tetrahydridocarbon.
>
> Methane can cause Asphyxia (a condition in which your body doesn't have enough oxygen causing unconsciousness, and sometimes death.

Therefore, methane is one very important mega block in Carbon Block Puzzle, but there are others too!

BLACK CARBON

Black carbon is a class of particles that are formally referred to as PM2.5. This means they are under 2.5 microns in diameter, or 0.0025 mm. One of the most well-known of them is soot. Black carbon is formed by the incomplete **combustion** of fuel. It's often produced with carbon monoxide. Though carbon monoxide is not a greenhouse gas, it can lead to death if not properly treated. Let's get back to black carbon. One of the things about black carbon is that it has a lifetime of only a few days to a few weeks. But this is not a reason not to worry about it, because it has significant direct and indirect effects on climate change, agriculture, and human health. The reason it can show this effect in such a short lifetime is because it is 460 to 1500 times stronger than CO_2 and fifty-two times stronger than methane. That's why another name for super pollutants is SLCPs, which is short for Short-Lived Climate Pollutants.

Black carbon prevents ice from forming by clinging onto the ice and absorbing heat from the sun, melting the ice. Most black carbon is released by household appliances. Most of this occurs in developing countries.

Black carbon impacts the lungs in a similar way to smoking. This is because of the size of black carbon. Black carbon can dim sunlight that reaches the earth, deposits on leaves and increases their temperature, and modifies climate patterns. It can disrupt monsoons, which are critical for agriculture and maintaining environmental stability. These effects are felt hard in Asia and Africa. Black carbon is very strong, so totally cutting black carbon emissions would delay climate change from passing the point at which there would be a runaway greenhouse effect. Overall, black carbon is a key mega block in climate change, and yes, it's the nastiest.

> **NOT-SO-FUN-FACT**
>
> The smallest particles of black carbon are the most harmful to the human body, because they can go the furthest into your lungs.
>
> The WHO estimates that about 7 million people die from black carbon each year.
>
> Respiratory diseases, cancer, cardiovascular (affecting the heart) diseases, and even birth defects are caused by black carbon.

HYDROFLUOROCARBONS (HFCS)

Hydrofluorocarbons are a group of chemicals primarily used for cooling. They were developed to replace ODSs (Ozone Depleting Substances) that were being phased out under the Montreal Protocol on substances that deplete the ozone layer. You might think they're very useful and help the environment with this introduction, but in fact, they are very powerful greenhouse gases. They have a lifetime between 15 to 29 years in the atmosphere, which is around the lifetime of methane. The Kigali amendment to cut the number of hydrofluorocarbons by more than 80% by 2050 was enacted in 2019. This would avoid a warming of 0.5º C, which could save the earth from going over the tipping point. The HFCs are one of the most powerful mega blocks because they are 1430 times as powerful as CO_2 and as mentioned earlier, they could stay up in the atmosphere for fifteen to twenty-nine years. In the end, hydrofluorocarbons are very powerful mega blocks and play an extremely important role in climate change.

NITROUS OXIDE (N_2O)

Nitrous oxide is one of the long-lived super pollutants. It stays in the atmosphere for an average of 144 years, meaning it can pack a punch for a long time. It contributes to 6% of all greenhouse gas emissions worldwide and when it is exposed to enough sunlight and oxygen it gets converted into nitrogen monoxide (NO), which breaks down the ozone layer. The ozone layer is the layer of the earth's atmosphere that protects life forms on earth from deadly UV rays (UV rays are the type that give you sunburns) from the sun. N_2O is 300 times more powerful than CO_2 over a 100-year timescale. Most of the N_2O comes from agriculture, mainly from fertilizers and water-logged soil. Cars without **catalytic converters** also release nitrous oxide. Wastewater treatment also generates N_2O. There are also some natural sources of it, but one of them is being accelerated by other greenhouse gases which makes something known as a **positive feedback loop**. When permafrost thaws, it releases methane and many other greenhouse gases, which thaw the permafrost even more, and the permafrost releases more greenhouse gases, thawing the permafrost even more, and so on.

There are many huge mega blocks, and more are coming! You might wonder, "What are we supposed to do with these blocks?" Well, you're about to find out!

5. DESTROY THE BLOCKS

NOW THAT YOU have a grip on just what the problem is, you'll definitely want to know how to prevent it. One person alone cannot prevent climate change. Instead, it takes all of the citizens of earth to stop climate change. Even though, you should do your part, as others will follow. Here are some ways to stop climate change at home.

LOWER ELECTRICITY USAGE

- Turn off lights when you don't need them.
- Always unplug devices when you're not using them (these devices are also known as **electricity vampires**. Coincidentally, PLUG spelled backward is GULP).
- Don't use screensavers.

- Use **ENERGY STAR** appliances.
- Use power strips.
- **Insulate** your home.
- Use microwave ovens rather than **convection ovens** (microwave ovens are four times as efficient as convection ovens).

> **SOMETHING TO THINK ABOUT**
>
> To remove all the CO_2 from the atmosphere each individual person in the world would have to remove one ton of CO_2 from the atmosphere.

CUT DOWN ON CARBON DIOXIDE

- Plant trees if you can.
- Ride a bike or walk when possible.
- Drive less.
- Use public transportation.
- Use renewable energy.
- Use electric, hybrid, and hydrogen fuel cell vehicles if you can.
- Take fewer short-haul flights.
- Buy locally grown foods.
- Buy used products.
- Reduce meat consumption.
- Recycle and opt-out of junk mail if you can.

Credit: nrdc.org
Food waste.

RETHINK FOOD WASTE

- The largest producer of methane is agriculture, specifically agricultural waste. As food decays and spoils, it emits methane.
- Buy food grown locally, because the further away food is grown, the further vehicles have to transport it, and, therefore the more carbon dioxide is released.
- Eat less cow meat, because cows' digestive systems release methane, which contributes to climate change.
- Grow your food. There is no transportation required and plants take in carbon dioxide and release oxygen.
- Buy food with less packaging as the process of making it releases lots of greenhouse gases.

- Compost food scraps. According to the EPA, (Environmental Protection Agency) approximately 18 % of methane emissions come from food scraps.

SAVE WATER

- Fix leaks and drips.
- Install low-flow showerheads.
- Put **aerators** on faucets.

> **DID YOU KNOW?**
>
> US refrigerators annually consume the energy equivalent of 25 huge power plants.

- The clean water pumped to most houses in North America has been treated, which uses a lot of energy. When we use less water, we use less energy, so our carbon footprint decreases.
- Use water-efficient faucets, **fixtures**, and appliances.
- Use a rain barrel to collect water for watering plants.
- Turn off faucets when they are not being used.
- Take shorter showers
- Use washing machines only on a full load.

> **DID YOU KNOW?**
>
> Cutting 4 minutes off your shower can save 20 gallons of water.

- Install toilets that only use 1.6 gallons or less per flush.

Credit: https://populationmatters.org
Tonnes of CO_2 saved per person per year undertaking each action.

Now, you see that climate change is an issue you can help prevent at home but keep this in mind: you are just destroying a few of the blocks. One person alone can't win the game, but still, let's destroy the blocks. You'd still help prevent us from reaching the point where we're at **GAME OVER!**

NOT-SO-FUN-FACTS

Running the faucet while brushing your teeth can waste 4 gallons of water.

Dripping faucets waste more than 1000 gallons per year.

In the US, we spend 61 billion dollars each year buying clean, bottled water.

6. GAME OVER

I'M SURE YOU want to know a good reason why you should read this book. You probably read all the previous chapters mainly because you want to know what happens if you reach **GAME OVER**. That's what you'll find out in this chapter.

WEATHER

Changes in Precipitation Patterns

Average precipitation will vary greatly due to rapid changes in temperature. Projections of future climate say that rainfall will be capricious. Some areas will be struggling to get the water the water they need, but the rest will be getting more water than they can handle.

Flooding

Coastal cities around the globe are facing severe flooding due to sea level rise and torrential rain. In one century, the sea level might rise by one meter. Unfortunately, these coastal cities tend to be the most populated. For example, Jakarta, the capitol city of Indonesia, is in danger of disappearing under the sea by 2050. Due to this, the Indonesian government is planning to move their capitol city to East Kalimantan by 2024.

Louisiana Floods
Credit: FEMA

Heatwaves and Droughts

California Drought
Dry River Bed
Credit: https://www.americanrivers.org

Most of the previous years have had record highs in temperature. Soil is becoming much less moist, and the temperature is rising fast.

Droughts are long periods of low humidity and high heat. They tend to occur inland.

Heatwaves are periods of high heat that stretch from days to weeks. Heatwaves are caused by trapped air that is warmed to extreme heat by sunlight. Heatwaves in Europe have been devastating, for example, in France, one heatwave killed 1,000 plus people in 2019. Extreme summer heat happens about 7% of the time now.

ECOSYSTEMS AND HABITATS

Food Redistribution

As the climate changes, areas of perfect growing conditions will become less common. This also means that the areas where crops can be grown will frequently change.

Displacement

While the temperature rises, animals that require lower temperatures are driven to higher and higher elevations. This leads to much more competition, making it harder to survive. This reduces the amount of habitable space, which allows fewer animals. When the temperature rises high enough, animals will reach the point where they can't go any higher and go extinct if they don't adapt. Some examples of the creatures that have been affected by this are pikas, animals that depend on sea ice, and cold-water fish.

Habitat Loss

As the climate changes and the temperature rises this will eradicate many habitats because the conditions for them aren't favorable. Firstly, the temperature could be too high for certain habitats. For example, the Arctic ice sheets are melting very rapidly. Changes in precipitation will completely destroy habitats in ways such as major flooding and droughts. People destroy huge swaths of land to create room for their utilities such as farmland and houses. CO_2 is making water more acidic, which is harming corals and bleaching them (coral bleaching). It's also causing creatures' shells to dissolve, which could cause a mass extinction that would wipe out two-thirds of all sea life. Climate change is one of the major causes of extinction. According to the IPCC, 20% to 30% of plant and animal species evaluated so far in climate change studies are at risk of extinction if climate change proceeds at this rate until the end of the century.

NOT-SO-FUN-FACTS

- 3.5 million deaths per year were caused by water-related diseases.

- 800,000 hectares of mangroves are lost every year. Mangroves store up to 10 times as much carbon per hectare as tropical forests.

- Since 1870, global sea levels have risen by about 8 inches.

- The worst impacts of climate change could be irreversible by 2030.

- The 20 warmest years on the record have been in the last 22 years (as of September 2020).

- 2/3rd of extreme weather events in the last 20 years were influenced by climate change, though no single storm is caused only by climate change.

- Dengue fever could spread through much of the south-eastern US by 2050.

- There is more CO_2 in the atmosphere now than at any time in human history.

HEALTH IMPACTS

Smog is one of the health impacts on people caused by climate change. It's created when you have an extreme amount of air pollution. It can harm your lungs if inhaled. In Beijing, China, smog polluted the air, making it toxic, which means people can't go outside. Some beetles get benefited from climate change and started taking down trees, such as wood-boring beetles. Lyme disease, which is transmitted by ticks, has become more common because as the temperature rises, its range expands northward.

Higher concentrations of CO_2 in the atmosphere can lower the nutrition in crops. Extreme temperature and precipitation can increase the number of pathogens on plants.

We are at a critical point, a threshold where if we don't act, it is game over. It's not just game over for us, because we are playing **ONE FOR ALL!**

DID YOU KNOW?

Air pollution can increase your susceptibility to coronavirus because air pollution can cause respiratory diseases which can make you an easy target for COVID-19.

7. ONE FOR ALL

SINCE WE CHOSE to play one for all, if we lose, everything we know and cherish will be gone. But what will be their plight? That's what you're about to find out.

As the temperature increases across the world, animals are pushed to the poles and higher elevations. The American pika is a great example. Its range is being driven up mountains to escape the heat. Because of the heat, spring temperatures have been reached earlier, meaning the birds lay their eggs earlier than usual. Flowers bloom earlier and mammals come out of **hibernation** sooner. Animal species begin moving towards the poles to escape higher temperatures [refer to sub-topic displacement on page 34].

As the temperatures rise, winters come later. This was surely to the plight of the polar bear. During the summer months, polar bears must live off the fat they gained in winter hunting in on the ice. Polar bears rarely hunt on land, so polar bears would starve if winter comes too late. This is a stunning case of how something as simple as ice melting could cause majestic polar bears to starve.

In 1980, Hudson Bay polar bears were strong, large, and well-fed. By 2016, they have lost lots of weight and become weaker. Since they have less time on ice, their hunting season has become shorter, which means they have less food. In Hudson Bay, the number of polar bears has reduced and there are fewer cubs. In 2016, the water in Hudson Bay didn't freeze until December 12, even though usually it freezes over in early November.

Credit:green peace / twitter - dailymail.co.uk
Polar bear comparison - 2009 vs 2019

Because of climate change, habitats are becoming fragmented, breaking up into much less diverse environments. **Homeothermic** (warm-blooded) animals will have to use more energy to regulate their temperature as climate changes. Conditions will become better for vector-borne diseases and parasites in different areas.

The snow leopard's habitat is being destroyed by people because of the conditions of their area changing. The giant panda feeds almost exclusively on bamboo and bamboo forests are being destroyed. This leaves the pandas to starve. The monarch butterfly is very heavily dependent on the environment for cues for reproduction, migration, and hibernation. There was a 53% decrease in the area occupied by monarch butterflies. Since the climate is changing, it's hard for monarch butterflies to notice when to reproduce, migrate or hibernate. Sea turtles are very sensitive to temperature changes. Whether a baby sea turtle is a male or female is determined by the temperature of the egg.

As the temperature rises, more sea turtles are females than males, which could lead to a drop in the sea turtle population.

An African elephant needs between forty and eighty gallons of fresh water a day for drinking, and droughts are becoming much more common, making it harder for elephants to find water. Mountain gorillas are stuck in a very small range surrounded by human settlements, so they can't move anywhere else, so they are on the endangered species list.

The African elephants eat local grass and plants that invasive species are eating to extinction, so it's hard for them to find food. The cheetah has very low **genetic diversity** and has a very low ability to adapt to rapidly changing environments.

Due to climate change, the water has become so acidic it is dissolving sea creatures' shells. It can also bleach corals. This is happening to the world's largest coral reef, the Great Barrier Reef. This has happened in two years in a row — 2016 and 2017. If this is the present, what is the future?

Since we played one for all, everything we cherish is in our hands. If we fail, nothing will ever be the same again. Not only this, now we've **leveled up**!

> **NOT-SO-FUN-FACT**
>
> The Bramble Cay melomy is the first mammal to go extinct because of climate change.
>
> More than 1 million species are at risk of extinction by climate change.
>
> Humanity has wiped out 60% of animal population since 1970.
>
> Less than 2% of polar bear hunts are successful. Polar bears can't reliably catch seals in open water.
>
> 40% of the world's bird species are in decline and 1 in 8 is threatened with global extinction.
>
> Due to habitat loss and poaching the Sumatran rhinos are on the verge of extinction with less than 75 remaining in the world.

8. LEVEL UP

WE JUST LEVELED up. Exponentially more blocks are being placed. If you look at the graphs, you'll see that the rate of CO_2 emissions is increasing. As of Dec 2020, CO_2 levels reached 414.75 ppm (parts per million). Why does this concentration matter? If you go back to chapter 6, you would get a pretty good idea of why. If you look at any source of CO_2 concentration across the world stretching back throughout the earth's history, you would see a series of large changes in the amount of CO_2 in the air, but then at the end, you would see a huge peak in CO_2 concentrations. That huge peak is man-made climate change. Since CO_2 is a large component of climate change, you would see that when CO_2 concentration increases, the temperature increases.

Carbon Block Puzzle

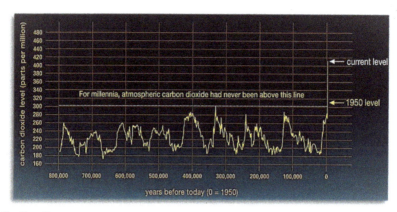

Credit: climate.nasa.gov

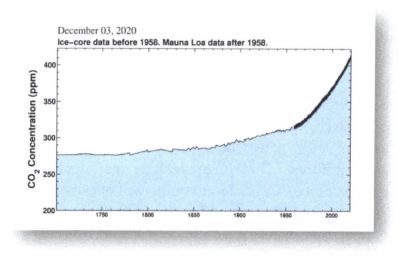

Credit: SCRIPPS INSTITUTION OF OCEANOGRAPHY

WHAT IS OUR PATH?

Global Temperature Rise

Global temperature is a major indicator of climate change. As of 2019, the temperature was 0.98 degrees Celsius (1.97 degrees Fahrenheit) above average. 19 of the 20 warmest years on record have occurred since 2001. The only year warmer than those after 2001 on record was 1998. Overall, 2020 was the warmest year of all with a temperature of 2.11 degrees Fahrenheit, and remember, usually global temperature measurements (such as the ones above) are showing the temperature above the twentieth-century average. February 2020 marked the 44th consecutive February, and 42nd consecutive month reaching temperatures above the twentieth-century average. It also holds the record for the warmest February without an El Niño.

NOT-SO-FUN-FACT

A snow-free winter caused ski resorts to close in Washington in 2004.

By 2050, over half the estimated world population of 9.5 billion will face water shortage.

Burning a gallon of gasoline emits almost 20 lbs of CO_2.

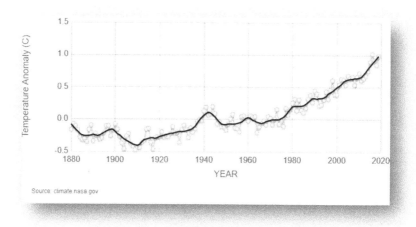

Credit: NASA/GISS– Global Temperature Anomaly

You can see one effect of this, melting sea ice and snow cover in extremely large amounts. The portion of the Arctic Ocean covered in sea ice in 2018 is only 66% of the size it used to be in 1979. This is a major indicator that we have *LEVELED UP!*

Humanity

As the human population increases rapidly, greenhouse gases get released more rapidly. What happens is that more and more people want new technologies, and therefore, more and more greenhouse gases are being released. This means if you want to continue the trend of our rising population, we need to lower our **carbon footprint** by a greater amount than the rate at which the population is rising. The fact that the population is rising implies we must use lots more resources from the environment, emit a lot more greenhouse gases, and we need more space, which means we must cut down more trees, which eliminates carbon sinks and releases lots of CO_2. This also reduces the habitats of other animals.

Getting, using, and disposing of resources (like coal, iron, and wood, etc.,) uses a lot of energy and can require machines that release greenhouse gases, so overall global warming is closely tied with population and usage of resources.

The more blocks are placed, the harder it is to beat the game.

NOT-SO-FUN-FACT

Dengue fever infects about 400 million people every year. The IPCC projects that the rise in temperatures could put 5 to 6 billion people at risk of contracting dengue fever by the 2080s, which is close to our current population as of 2020.

A 1 degree Celsius increase in temperature is associated with a 4.27% increase in cardiovascular disease mortality.

Table 6.1: Examples of how diverse environmental changes affect the occurrence of various infectious diseases in humans (Refernce 5)

Environmental changes	Example diseases	Pathway of effect
Dams, canals, irrigation	Schistosomiasis	▲ Snail host habitat, human contact
	Malaria	▲ Breeding sites for mosquitoes
	Helminthiasies	▲ Larval contact due to moist soil
	River blindness	▼ Blackfly breeding, ▼ disease
Agricultural intensification	Malaria	Crop insecticides and ▲ vector resistance
	Venezuelan haemorraghic fever	▲ rodent abundance, contact
Urbanization, urban crowding	Cholera	▼ sanitation, hygiene; ▲ water contamination
	Dengue	Water-collecting trash, ▲ Aedes aegypti mosquito breeding sites
	Cutaneous leishmaniasis	▲ proximity, sandfly vectors
Deforestation and new habitation	Malaria	▲ Breeding sites and vectors, immigration of susceptible people
	Oropouche	▲ contact, breeding of vectors
	Visceral leishmaniasis	▲ contact with sandfly vectors
Reforestation	Lyme disease	▲ tick hosts, outdoor exposure
Ocean warming	Red tide	▲ Toxic algal blooms
Elevated precipitation	Rift valley fever	▲ Pools for mosquito breeding
	Hantavirus pulmonary syndrome	▲ Rodent food, habitat, abundance

▲ increase   ▼ reduction

Credit: WHO – Environment Change vs Diseases

Diseases

After the COVID-19 pandemic, it should be pretty easy for people to understand how devastating diseases can be. Outbreaks are becoming much more frequent because people are taking up more space, which means we are coming in closer contact with animals, which can allow viruses to transmit from animals to people more easily. Respiratory diseases that come from really small particles will become much more common because lots more PM 2.5 (black carbon) molecules will be released into the atmosphere. Air pollution will increase dramatically due to climate change, which would create lots of smog, which can harm people. Countless diseases caused by air pollution are undoubtedly becoming a lot more common. Diseases are a major threat to the world (yes, even to animals!) all because of climate change.

Even though we've leveled up and more blocks are being placed, the worst of things will only come if we take the path where we continue the rising trend of carbon dioxide emissions. We still have a chance to **WIN THE GAME**!

Carbon Block Puzzle

9. WINNING THE GAME

THOUGH THERE ARE ways to impede climate change that you can do every day on your own, that won't be enough to stop climate change. That doesn't mean you shouldn't do these things, but these bigger solutions are the only way to stop climate change fully.

Here is a list of some ways to stop climate change:

We can pedestrianize streets by only allowing **pedestrians** on them. One example is the city of Ghent, Belgium, where only people and trams can use the streets. A city on the base of the Matterhorn called Zermatt, Switzerland has no cars at all. Primary vehicles can access a small town called Täsch, which is 5 kilometers away from Zermatt. Then, you have to take trains to the city. Inside the city, you can easily move around on foot, horse-drawn carriage, e-taxi, bike, or an e-bus.

You can also try to increase the green performance of buildings by setting goals for them and taking steps to achieve them.

People can advocate for better building codes, energy efficiency. The better a building code, the more energy-efficient the building would be.

Cities could begin using 100% clean energy so that way fewer greenhouse gases are emitted.

Cities should support a **carbon tax**, which is a fee imposed on burning fossil fuels. It's a way to pay for the protection of Earth from climate change. It also motivates companies to switch to renewable energy.

Corporate sustainability initiatives should be supported to increase the efficiency of large companies and if possible, we should try to start one by ourselves.

DID YOU KNOW?

Portugal is powered completely by renewable energy.

Renewable energy creates 5 times more jobs than fossil fuels.

Iceland is the world's largest green energy producer per capita. 100% of Iceland's energy is supplied by geothermal and hydropower energy.

The world's largest dam, the Itaipu dam provides electricity for both Brazil and Paraguay.

As of 2017, China builds 2 wind turbines every hour.

Cities could be built with denser and higher buildings to decrease the number of trees cut down and increase the space used in the city.

Promote offsetting of carbon emissions for companies and even cities. This means to utterly neutralize cities' **carbon footprints** and try to remove carbon dioxide from the atmosphere to reverse climate change.

Invest in community solar projects and work with them. This allows communities to run a shared solar installation. In fact, in New York City, the Brooklyn microgrid is trying to create a market to sell local energy between neighbors.

Regenerative Farming

One way to help win the game is to use regenerative farming. Soil stores carbon. Plants and other organisms can help the soil store more carbon. Conventional farming usually involves tilling. Tilling can disrupt topsoil, which produces runoff and makes it hard for the soil to store carbon. Conventional farming eliminates biodiversity which not only reduces crop resilience but also reduces the soil's ability to take in CO_2 and store it. Regenerative farming on the other hand mimics nature.

It allows livestock to graze in a controlled way. This prevents the grass from being overgrazed. Livestock feces can help the plants be grown in controlled amounts.

With this method, the grass has enough time to recover before it is grazed on again. This allows the grass and the other crops to capture more CO_2 from the atmosphere than they would with conventional farming.

RENEWABLE ENERGY

Solar Power

Renewable energy is one of the best sources of power if we want to stop climate change. One of the most well-known sources of renewable energy is solar power, which runs on energy from the sun. One of the major drawbacks of solar power is that it requires a specific temperature range to operate successfully and a huge space. We should use solar power since it doesn't release as many greenhouse gases as coal and other fossil fuels.

> **DID YOU KNOW?**
>
> In August 2015, the first solar power plane (The Solar Impulse) flew around the world without using a single drop of fossil fuel.
>
> The world's first solar power satellite was called Vanguard 1 and it was launched in 1958. It is still in orbit now.
>
> There are nearly 5,500 schools around the US, using solar power technologies.
>
> An elementary school in Bowling Green, Kentucky is using solar panels to power its classrooms, gyms, and cafeteria. This is the first Net Zero school.

There are two different ways to capture the sun's energy

1. Solar thermal technology
2. Photovoltaics

Solar thermal power uses reflective mirrors and dark surfaces, while photovoltaics use solar panels. Sunlight is composed of photons, which are tiny particles that carry solar energy, which comes in very specific amounts, called **quanta**. The first solar cell was created in 1954 by three scientists at Bell Laboratories in New Jersey. It was made from 2 silicon plates put very close together. They produce electricity when photons strike the first silicon plate and send electrons to the second silicon plate, which generates an electric current.

This form of renewable energy can help stop climate change by providing an alternative to fossil fuels that you can install in your home. The second type of solar power is solar thermal energy, and it splits into two different types; concentrated solar power and passive solar power. Concentrated solar power uses mirrors to reflect a large amount of sunlight onto a very small area. The mirrors will move around to follow the sun throughout the day. The concentrated light heats water and evaporates it into steam, which powers a generator, creating electricity. Passive solar energy is a simple system that involves a dark surface that heats water for uses inside a house which has some of the same benefits as using solar cells. Solar energy might have some drawbacks. We can't constantly get enough sunlight in most highly populated cities, which need electricity the most, but there are large areas where we can find enough sunlight. That's why solar energy can help to win this game of Carbon Block Puzzle.

Wind Energy

Wind energy relies on building taller, larger turbines. This is because the larger the turbine, the more wind it captures, and the higher up the turbines, the stronger the wind. The best thing about wind energy is it's everywhere and it's constant but varying. Wind is caused by cooler, denser air being pulled toward warmer, less dense air. The area once filled with high-density air now has low-density air. The area with high density now has low-density which recreates the current and sends the air back to its starting point, creating a **convection current**. Windmills were the first to harness this energy. Some of the earliest windmills were used to pump water. Today's wind turbines use wind to generate electricity. A wind turbine has large blades, which spin a shaft, which powers a generator. This is how wind power works. The basic principle behind the wind turbine is **Bernoulli's law**, which creates lift on wings. Each of these blades is like a small wing that spins the shaft when wind hits it. Wind turbines can be installed virtually in any location, since wind occurs everywhere, just in varying amounts. There is another type of energy similar to wind

> **DID YOU KNOW?**
>
> One wind turbine can generate enough electricity to power 1400 homes.
>
> Towns county school in Hiawassee, Georgia is using a wind turbine to power their school campus.

energy, which is a form of hydroelectric energy that is powered by underwater currents, which generate electricity in the same way as wind turbines. They are also a bit more accessible, especially to coastal cities.

Wind energy is going to be another chance to win the game.

Hydroelectric Energy

Hydroelectric energy is full of possibilities. For example, there are hydroelectric turbines. The best thing is, we can get them practically anywhere, since water is everywhere and it's always moving. Hydroelectric power uses the energy of moving water to produce electricity. The energy of moving water is hydrokinetic. Hydrokinetic energy accounts for about 50% of all renewable energy generators. One type of device that makes hydroelectric energy is something known as an Anaconda, which harnesses wave energy to produce electricity. It is a 200-meter-long hollow rubber cylinder filled with fresh water that's anchored just below the surface of the water. When waves hit the sea surface, a bulge runs through the Anaconda at the same speed as the wave, and the bulge eventually pushes the inside water through a turbine, which generates electricity. There are also buoy systems made from neodymium (a magnetic material) that will rise and fall with the tides and waves and move across some carpet wire, which will generate electricity. There are also tidal turbines which are like wind turbines, but they harness the rising and falling of the tides.

One of the greatest advantages of hydroelectric energy is that it is very easily accessible and can be placed in a very large range. It also provides energy constantly, whether it's day or night, stormy or calm (although the amount of energy produced will vary). The best thing of all is that it is a fantastic way to wean the world off of fossil fuels.

Geothermal Energy

It harnesses the heat from the core of the earth and uses it to boil water, then the steam spins a turbine to power a generator. The **oceanic crust** of the ocean is much thinner than the **continental crust**, which is over land. This means it is easier to access the heat of the earth in the ocean. This would mean you can build a geothermal plant underwater, where you would have access to a huge amount of water, which would allow you to save a huge amount of electricity by not having to transport the water. You can also use geothermal pumps for powering your air conditioning and heating in your house. This system works because of the fact that in the summer, it is cool a few feet underground, whereas, in winter, it's much warmer at the same depth. The system simply uses a pipe put underground to cool off the water in summer and heat the water in winter. The nation of Costa Rica has been running on 100% renewable energy and planning to become carbon neutral nation by the end of 2021.

Geothermal energy is a major player as it can produce a constant supply of energy that can be used for a very long time and can be put in a wide variety of places.

Carbon Block Puzzle

All these types of renewable energy cannot stop climate change on their own. Here are two types of energy that may not be renewable but are still a powerful way to eliminate the blocks by placing them in the right places.

Biofuel Energy

If we look at wind, solar, and hydropower, they are all powered by the sun. But they aren't the only sources of energy that harnesses the sun's energy. There are many types of biofuel such as ethanol, biodiesel, biomass, and biogas (methane). Plants use the sun's energy to grow through a process called **photosynthesis**, which takes energy from the sun and uses it to convert carbon dioxide and water into **glucose** with the waste product of oxygen. When other animals eat the plants, they absorb one-tenth of the energy the plant has.

> **DID YOU KNOW?**
>
> Ethanol is produced through the fermentation of biomass that is high in carbohydrates such as sugarcane, wheat, and corn. As of 2012, Brazil and the US were the largest producers of Ethanol and Bio-diesel in the world.

To make biofuels you need to convert the sugars found in plants into usable energy, which is biofuel. One of the earliest forms of biomass is wood.

Until the mid-1800s, wood was the primary source of energy. In fact, we occasionally use wood for energy today too. Nowadays solid biomass is used in the form of briquettes, pellets, and charcoal.

In 1986, Barre Town middle and elementary school in Barre, Vermont decided to install a woodchip boiler to heat their school, which saved them millions of dollars. In 2013 alone biofuel helped provide about 5% of energy in the US.

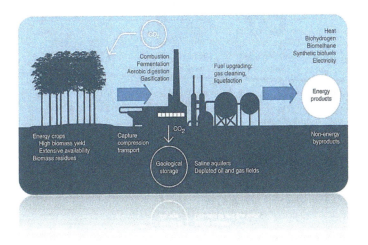

Credit: Diagram courtesy of Nature
The process of converting biomass into electricity and fuels and capturing and storing the carbon emissions.

Carbon Block Puzzle

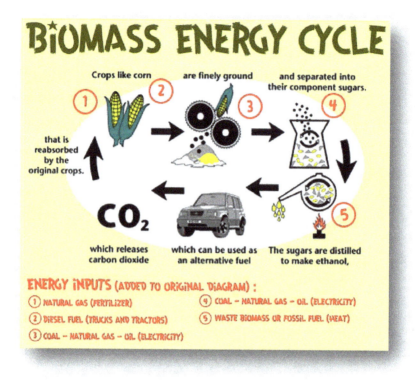

Credit: ihsph.org– Biomass Energy Cycle.

Nuclear Energy

Nuclear energy runs on uranium fuel rods which are surrounded by water. After the water is pumped in, the uranium atoms will begin to split, creating heat, which boils the water, sending it up through a tube with a turbine that powers the generator as the steam runs through it.

Nuclear energy is constant. We have control over it when it's made. The downside of nuclear energy is it produces toxic nuclear waste and if the fuel rods melt, they will go through the bottom of the container and cause a nuclear meltdown. Though nuclear energy isn't considered renewable, it will help lead the way to stop climate change as it provides an alternative for fossil fuels.

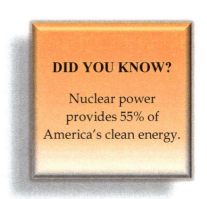

DID YOU KNOW?

Nuclear power provides 55% of America's clean energy.

CARBON CAPTURE

Carbon capture is one way to remove CO_2 from the atmosphere. There are three main techniques of carbon capture.

1. Post Combustion Carbon Capture
2. Pre Combustion Carbon Capture
3. Oxy-fuel Combustion Carbon Capture

Direct Air Capture

Direct Air Capture (DAC) uses fans to suck in air and separate CO_2 as a gas. It uses chemical processes to separate the CO_2. Direct air capture is efficient but very expensive. To be specific it costs $250 - $600 per ton. It is also very energy intensive.

So where does the CO₂ go?

Now that the CO2 is extracted from the air, we need to put it somewhere. It is usually stored underground and sometimes it is reused to make fuel for cars. Yep! That's right. The very fuel whose remnants that we are trying so hard to get out of the atmosphere. Either way these solutions are either carbon neutral or carbon negative. I think it may be possible to split the CO_2 into carbon and oxygen and use the carbon for building structures and release the oxygen into the atmosphere in the future.

Carbon captures plays a critical part in preventing and reversing climate change.

WINNING THE GAME

There are many sources of renewable energy to win the game. They are all said to replace fossil fuels, but they can't replace fossil fuels all by themselves. They need someone to play!

10. LOOK WHO IS PLAYING

CARBON BLOCK PUZZLE CAN BE hard, but it's practically impossible if you're not actively playing. One thing that is on our side is that there are a lot of people playing with impressive skills. Scientists, researchers, companies, organizations, and even normal people are working on ways to win this game of Carbon Block Puzzle.

COMPANIES

One of the leading companies stopping climate change is Microsoft, which sets its renewable energy portfolio (the amount of renewable energy to be used) to 1900 megawatts, which could power 1.5 million US homes.

Google bought 1.6 GW of renewable energy, which made its total clean energy portfolio big enough to power Uruguay. Another example is McDonald's, which got 380 MW in renewable energy, which is equivalent to taking 140,000 cars off the road for one year, which reduces the block already known as a major culprit of climate change. Walmart, environmental groups, and over 1000 suppliers worked on the initiative "project gigaton", which works to remove a billion tons of greenhouse gas pollution from the company's global supply chain by 2030.

Tyson Foods partnered up with an environmental group known as pro forest to reduce deforestation by measuring the risk of it. Kohl's went carbon neutral (no carbon dioxide emissions) from 2010 to 2014 and they were close to meeting it in 2015. Kohl's has been named the top green power using retailer in the US ever since 2009. The tech giant Apple's headquarters is

DID YOU KNOW?

Google's HQ in Silicon Valley is powered by 100% renewable energy, which removes an estimated 5 million tonnes of CO_2 from the atmosphere.

In 2018, LEGO launched its first sustainable bricks, made from sugarcane-based plastic.

There are around 550,000 TESLA cars on the road, which have so far prevented 4 million tonnes of CO_2 from entering the atmosphere.

In 2019, Dell Inc., committed to making its plastic trays in laptop boxes from 25% ocean plastics and 75% other recycled plastics, diverting 16000 lbs of plastics from the oceans.

powered 100% by renewable energy. Apple already powered 100% of its operations in the US, China, and 21 other countries with renewable energy. The Ray Foundation in Georgia is another organization that is working on stopping climate change. It is testing solar roads, solar-powered vehicle charging stations, and smart roads on an 18 mile stretch of West Georgia's I-85. They are also trying to set up miles of native pollinator gardens in the roadways to help protect water systems from roadside pollution.

SCIENTISTS

Dr. Joseph Romm

Dr. Joseph Romm is an American author, physicist, climate scientist, and editor. He advocated to stop global warming and increase energy security using increased energy efficiency, green energy, and green transportation.

Dr. Joseph Romm

Dr. Joseph Romm said that changes in the earth's orbit known as **Milankovitch cycles** should be making the earth cool down very slowly, whereas, in reality, it's warming very fast, which is instant proof of climate change. He also wrote the books *Climate Change: What Everyone Needs to Know, Hell and High Water, The Hype about Hydrogen,* and *Fact and Fiction in the Race to Save the Climate.*

Svante Arrhenius

In the 1890s, the Swedish scientist Svante Arrhenius and his coworker Arvind Hogborn thought that carbon dioxide from factories could be making a difference in the temperature. Using a bit of math, Arrhenius made the first climate model to predict how temperature would rise with greater greenhouse gas emissions. According to his model, if carbon dioxide increased to 2.5 to 3 times the level it was at the time, the temperature in the Arctic would rise about eight to nine degrees Celsius. Basically, he argued that man-made carbon dioxide greatly influenced the earth's temperature. In 1903, he earned the Nobel Prize in chemistry for the theory of electrolytic disassociation.

Roger Revelle

Roger Revelle was a scientist and scholar. Roger Revelle was one of the early scientists to study global warming, as well as the movement of the earth's tectonic plates. He discovered that oceans had a limit to how much carbon dioxide they could take in and that they took in carbon dioxide much more slowly than previously thought. He earned many awards and honors such as the National Medal of Science and the Tyler Prize for Environmental achievement, just to name a few. After he made his discovery, it became important to measure the earth's carbon dioxide levels. He has written the books *Energy and Climate,* and *Oceanography, Population Resources and the World.*

Charles David Keeling

Charles David Keeling was a scientist and oceanographer who first alerted the world to human contribution to climate change, which is known as "anthropogenic (man-made) global warming" He developed ways to measure carbon dioxide levels in the air.

Charles David Keeling

He purposely did this far away from cities which removes the effect of a heat island, which is when in a city, the buildings reflect and concentrate heat. In honor of him, the chart used to measure carbon dioxide level was called the Keeling Curve. The Keeling Curve measures the atmospheric carbon dioxide concentration in parts per million. If you look at the chart, the curve is very jagged. This is because seasonal changes in plant growth cause changes in the amount of carbon dioxide taken from the air, which therefore causes the curve to be jagged. His research also shows that there has been an increase in seasonal variation with samples in the late 20th century and early 21st century. Together with the IPCC (Intergovernmental Panel on Climate Change), he won the 2007 Nobel Peace Prize.

William E. Rees

William E. Rees created the ecological footprint, which is a measurement of the impact of humans on the environment. Later, the carbon footprint concept was born out of the ecological footprint.

William Armstrong

William Armstrong is the inventor of hydroelectric power. It was invented in 1878, six years before the modern steam turbine was invented.

Edmond Becquerel

Edmond Becquerel invented solar power it in 1839 The 19-year-old physicist discovered the photovoltaic effect when he shined a light on an electrode submerged in a conductive solution and it made electricity. He couldn't explain why though.

Charles Brush

Charles Brush invented the wind turbine in 1988. He used his turbine to charge a dozen batteries with 34 cells each. He used these batteries to power his house.

Jerry Whitfield

Jerry Whitfield invented biomass generation. Due to the scarcity of petroleum-based fuels in the early 1970s, aviation giant Boeing looked to fuel efficiency engineer Jerry Whitfield. He worked with Ken Tucker to build biomass pellets.

Now that you know how many people are playing Carbon Block Puzzle, all that's left to do is join in and make others do the same! Now that we know how to play the game, we're **IN IT TO WIN IT**!

11. IN IT TO WIN IT

BY NOW YOU know everything you need to know. You have what you need to have. You know how to play Carbon Block Puzzle. Now you just have to play by taking action. Now we all know why to play, so let the game begin.

Just know this one thing: we will not fail because we are in it to win it. What you choose to do will affect humanity and most of all, the next generation. We are the only hope for the next generation and the generations beyond that. If we make one wrong step, our fate is sealed. But we come back to this one question at all times: why are we doing this? We are doing this for humanity, for anything less than the best is unethical.

Now, you will gain from stopping climate change. You would get a wider variety of food. Food prices would go down. Humanity would be more connected with nature. We would have fewer natural disasters. We would overall feel better. Don't get me wrong, but none of these, in my opinion, are a good enough reason to stop climate change. Here is the real reason: the future of our civilization depends on it.

All of humanity is at stake. People will begin fighting for resources. The world would become like something out of a **dystopian** sci-fi novel. The only trace of civilization that we would leave would be crumbled buildings and an overheated planet. Do you want the next generation and those after that to live in this destroyed world? But they will not because we will take action! Civilization has stood up to every problem it has faced and will continue to do so. We are not going to let this vision of the world happen.

So, tread carefully because the consequences are immense. Many people are hiding from the truth like a little child hiding under the cover of their bed. If you faced something threatening the world, would you go to bed and pull up the covers? No, you would not. We are facing something threatening the world so we will rise against it, and when we rise, nothing can defeat us!

Homo Sapiens means "wise man". Sure, we may be smart. We have invented so many things but look at what we have done to nature. We have taken billions of years of evolution and destroyed it in less than 200 years. If you are wise, you don't just think smart, you listen. For 200 years, we have been deaf to Mother Nature's cries for help. We have been blind to all of the signs of Mother Earth's despair. According to me, we've been doing this two hundred years too many. Let's destroy the blocks while we can. If you want the one best reason to stop climate change, it's not for personal gain or preserving nature. It's for **morale** and **ethicality**. If a person single-handedly destroyed the Earth, that would be entirely unethical. In fact, it wouldn't be **humane**. But humanity is doing just that. If we destroy the Earth, leave it successfully, and live on another planet instead, even though we might save humanity, we would live in shame, knowing that we destroyed our planet for a "better life". We cannot tolerate losing this game of Carbon Block Puzzle. And we will not lose it because we will fight back! **<u>WE ARE IN IT TO WIN IT</u>**!

MASTER THE GAME: MORE INFORMATION

SOME MORE THINGS YOU SHOULD KNOW ABOUT CARBON BLOCK PUZZLE:

- A huge amount of fossil fuel formed in the Carboniferous period because when the first trees grew, organisms at the time were not at all adapted to digesting the dead trees. Hence all the trees were buried underground and became coal.
- Around 90% of our energy comes from fossil fuels.
- 52% of black carbon emissions are from mobile sources, mainly trucks and 93% of that total is from diesel engines.
- Mexico set a goal of reducing black carbon emission by 51% by 2030.
- A DVD or VCR consumes about 5 watts even when it is powered off.
- Just one Google search is the equivalent of using a 60W bulb for 17 seconds.
- 800 million people (11% of the world population) are currently vulnerable to the impacts of climate change.

- California suffered its longest drought period from December 2011 to March 2019 (lasted for 8 years)
- In 1984 – 85 a long drought in Ethiopia and Sudan killed 450,000 people.
- Spain, Italy, and Greece have managed 2 – 3% annual reductions in CO_2 emissions.
- The country Tuvalu has the lowest carbon footprint in the world (Zero $Mtco_2$)
- US keeps more than 260,000 lbs of CO_2 out of the atmosphere by preserving an average acre of forest.
- In 1999, the West Nile virus transmitted by mosquitoes to humans first appeared in Western New York, after a drought followed by heavy rains.
- Costa Rica uses 100% renewable energy for electricity.
- In 1709, British Industrialist Abraham Darby invented a way of using coal to produce iron which begins the intense use of fossil fuels as an industrial energy source.
- In 1827, French mathematician Jean-Baptiste Joseph Fourier discovered the greenhouse effect.
- In 1863, Irish scientist John Tyndall published a paper describing how water vapor can act as a greenhouse gas.
- In 1967, US geophysicist Syukuro Manabe and Richard Wetherald devised an early computer model of global climate.
- In 1988, the UN asked for a high-level scientific assessment of climate change, which led to the establishment of (IPCC – Intergovernmental Panel on Climate Change).

- In 1988, American climate scientist James E. Hansen testified to Congress that "The greenhouse effect has been detected and is changing our climate now".
- In September 2020, nearly 100 major wildfires raged in the western US. They burned an area almost the size of Connecticut.
- Black carbon kills over eight million people per year.
- Pollen season is getting worse and longer due to an increase in temperature, stoking more plants to make pollen for a longer period of time.
- Climate change has been linked to age-related macular degeneration (AMD), an irreversible type of vision loss.
- In India on February 7, 2021, a glacier snapped under the pressure of a glacial lake, leading to a flash flood. It killed over a thousand people and many more are missing.

DAYS TO PLAY THE GAME

- **February 2nd** – World Wetland Day
- **February 27th** – International Polar Bear Day
- **March 3rd** – World Wildlife Day
- **March 18th** – Global Recycling Day
- **March 21st** – International Forest Day
- **March 22nd** – World Water Day
- **April 10th** – Arbor Day
- **April 22nd** – Earth Day
- **May 3rd to 9th** – International Composting Awareness Week
- **May 17th** – Endangered Species Day
- **May 22nd** - World Biodiversity Day
- **June 6th** – World Environment Day
- **June 8th** – World Oceans Day
- **June 17th** – World Day to Combat Desertification and Drought
- **June 21st** – International Climate Change Day
- **June 22nd** – World Rainforest Day
- **July 28th** – World Nature Conservation Day
- **July 31st** – World Ranger Day
- **August 2nd** – National Tree Day
- **August 15th** – National Honeybee Day
- **September 5th** – Amazon Rainforest Day
- **September 16th** – International Day for the preservation of the Ozone Layer
- **3rd Saturday of September** – World Cleanup Day
- **September 21st** – Zero Emissions Day
- **September 22nd** – Car-free Day
- **September 23rd** – Earth Overshoot Day

- **September 26th** - World Environmental Health Day
- **Last Sunday of September** – World River Day
- **First Monday of October** – World Habitat Day
- **First Wednesday of October** – Energy Efficiency Day
- **October 4th** – World Animal Day
- **October 13th** – International Day for Natural Disaster Reduction
- **Fourth Wednesday of October** – Sustainability Day
- **October 24th** – International Day of Climate Action
- **November 15th** – America Recycles Day
- **December 4th** – Wildlife Conservation Day
- **December 11th** – International Mountain Day
- **December (Variable Date)** – Ozone Action Day

AFTERWORD

There he stood, in a kindergarten classroom at the age of 5. You could tell that he was nervous and shy, but you could also tell he had a confidence about him that I had never seen in a 5-year-old before. Not many words were spoken when I first met Sirish as a kindergartener in my classroom. He entered the classroom very quiet, shy and reserved. But it did not take long to quickly learn that Sirish Subash was a 5-year-old that was one day going to leave a positive mark here on Earth. He was going to be a young man who would make a difference in our world and make a positive change.

Once Sirish became more comfortable around me, he began to open up and show his true knowledge and his true passion for learning as well as teaching others. He would draw pictures and write about wave currents, magnetic fields, and how different pollutions would affect our Earth. He was playing chess, building robots, and making electric current models that would light up a lightbulb. I was not sure what to do with him at first. Most 5-year-olds are learning to write their name, count to 100, and sound out CVC words. But, Sirish was teaching this kindergarten teacher new tricks! There was not one thing in the kindergarten curriculum that I needed to teach to Sirish. His knowledge was already much deeper and developed.

Sirish is the type of student that comes along once in a lifetime for most teachers. I am beyond honored to have had the opportunity to meet Sirish. He changed me as a teacher. He helped me become a better teacher to all students. I knew he was going places. I knew he was a change maker. I knew he was going to make a difference. I knew he was driven, motivated, passionate and here he is, writing his first book! WOW! What an accomplishment for this young man. I look forward to continuing to watch Sirish as he makes his mark and changes the world. The well-written book by an amazingly gifted 4th grader proves that Sirish is passionate about helping the Earth and making a difference today so that there is a tomorrow.

Sirish did a nice job taking a very serious subject and making it come to life with the connection to Block Puzzle game. Sirish starts by taking time to explain what Carbon Block Puzzle is and how it is affecting our planet, our climate, and humans and animals. How the individual blocks are playing a role in the destruction of our environmental ecosystem. How people are playing a role in the destruction of our environmental ecosystem. Sirish provides many different examples of the blocks that are causing our climate and environment to change in a negative way. He also shared several different ideas and suggestions to help reduce the carbon footprint that is being left on our Earth. I believe that Sirish believes that everyone is playing the game of Carbon Block Puzzle, whether they know it or not.

Additionally, Sirish wants everyone to know they have an important role or job to play in the game so that changes can be made to better our planet. Whether you are one person or a big company, Sirish shares many ideas and suggestions that can have a positive impact on the carbon footprint here on Earth. When anyone plays a game, the goal is to win. With Carbon Block Puzzle, Sirish is in it to win it and desires everyone to join the game as well with the same attitude, I am in it to win it! With this approach, there can be a positive change for our future generations here on Earth.

Sirish, be proud of your accomplishment, writing a book about a heavy topic and making it come to life for all to read, understand, and help make a difference for today, tomorrow, and the future. You are here on this Earth to make a difference and leave a positive mark. You are well on your way and I am beyond honored to know you and watch your leave your make. When I first met you at the age of 5, I knew you were going to be someone extra special, someone with amazing talents, and someone that is here to help others. Thank you for gifting me with your knowledge, your kindness, and your love! I look forward to watching you grow and watching you make a difference. Keep your head high, believe in yourself, and know you are a positive force making a difference.

Kathleen Gresham,

Educational Specialist.

GLOSSARY

Aerators - a piece of equipment that adds air to water.

Bernoulli's law - is the principle by which airplane wings work. The shape of the wings causes the air to be **denser** at the bottom than the top, causing the air on the bottom to push up, making the airplane lift. It states that the faster a fluid moves, the lower the pressure it has.

Carbon dioxide – A colorless, odorless gas formed when carbon combines with oxygen. It's the main greenhouse gas responsible for global warming.

Carbon footprint - the number of greenhouse gases—primarily carbon dioxide—released into the atmosphere by particular human activity.

Carbon sinks - a carbon sink is anything, natural or otherwise, that absorbs more carbon than it releases, and thereby lowers the concentration of CO_2.

Carbon tax - a tax on fossil fuels, especially those used by motor vehicles, intended to reduce the emission of carbon dioxide.

Carboniferous period - The Carboniferous is a geologic period and system that spans 60 million years from the end of the Devonian Period 358.9 million years ago, to the beginning of the Permian Period, 298.9 Mya.

Cardiovascular - relating to the heart and blood vessels.

Catalytic converters - a device incorporated in the exhaust system of a motor vehicle, containing a catalyst for converting pollutant gases into less harmful ones.

Combustion - the process of burning something

Continental crust - the relatively thick part of the earth's crust that forms the large landmasses. It is generally older and more complex than the oceanic crust.

Convection current - a process of heat transfer through a gas or liquid by bulk motion of hotter material into a cooler region.

Convection ovens - a cooking device that heats food by the circulation of hot air.

Coral bleaching - When water is too warm, corals will expel the algae (zooxanthellae) living in their tissues causing the coral to turn completely white. This is called coral bleaching.

Decomposers – a living thing that decomposes organic matter.

Dystopian - relating to or denoting an imagined state or society where there is great suffering or injustice.

Element – is a substance made entirely from one type of atom that cannot be broken into simpler substances by ordinary chemical processes.

Energy Star - are the same or better than standard products, only they use less energy. Since they use less energy, these products save money on the electricity bill and help protect the environment by causing fewer harmful emissions from power plants.

Ethicality - pertaining to or dealing with morals or the principles of morality; pertaining to right and wrong in conduct.

Fixtures - a piece of equipment or furniture that is fixed in position in a building or vehicle.

Genetic diversity - the total number of genetic characteristics in the genetic makeup of a species.

Glucose – a sugar that is the product of photosynthesis and is plant food.

Greenhouse Gases - Greenhouse gases are certain gases in the atmosphere (water vapor, carbon dioxide, nitrous oxide, and methane, for example) that trap energy from the sun.

Hibernation - Hibernation is a type of deep sleep some animals (like bears) go into during winter. Hibernation is like a long nap.

Homoeothermic - a mammal or bird, having a body temperature that is constant and largely independent of the temperature of its surroundings.

Humane - having or showing compassion or benevolence.

Insulate - to cover, line, or separate with a material that prevents or reduces the passage, transfer, or leakage of heat, electricity, or sound.

Malnutrition – lack of proper nutrition, caused by not having enough to eat or not being able to use the food that one eats.

Mangroves - Mangroves are a group of trees and shrubs that live in the coastal intertidal zone. Many mangrove forests can be recognized by their dense tangle of prop roots that make the trees appear to be standing on stilts above the water.

Meteorological - related to the study of weather patterns and predicting future weather

Migration - is the movement of either people or animals from one area to another.

Milankovitch cycles – the collective effects of changes in the climate caused by changes in the earth's orbit.

Monsoon - the seasonal wind of the Indian Ocean and southern Asia, blowing from the southwest in summer and from the northeast in winter. (in India and nearby lands) the season during which the southwest monsoon blows, commonly marked by heavy rains; rainy season.

Morale - the confidence, enthusiasm, and discipline of a person or group at a particular time.

Neodymium - A neodymium magnet (also known as NdFeB, NIB, or Neo magnet) is the most widely used type of rare-earth magnet. It is a permanent magnet made from an alloy of neodymium, iron, and boron to form the $Nd_2Fe_{14}B$ tetragonal crystalline structure.

Net Zero – To produce all the energy that is used (meaning electricity bill would be zero dollars)

Ocean Acidification – a reduction of the pH of the ocean over an extended period of time caused by the ocean absorbing carbon dioxide from the atmosphere.

Oceanic crust - is the uppermost layer of the oceanic portion of a tectonic plate.

Organic matter – is matter that has come from a recently living organism. It is capable of decay, or is the product of decay, or is composed of organic compounds.

Pathogen - A pathogen is usually defined as a microorganism that causes, or can cause, disease. We have defined a pathogen as a microbe that can cause damage in a host.

Pedestrian - a person walking along a road or in a developed area.

Photosynthesis - the process by which green plants and some other organisms use sunlight to synthesize foods from carbon dioxide and water. Photosynthesis in plants generally involves the green pigment chlorophyll and generates oxygen as a byproduct.

Pollinator - A pollinator is an animal that moves pollen from the male anther of a flower to the female stigma of a flower.

Positive feedback loop – a process in which the end products of an action cause more of that action to occur in a feedback loop, causing small disturbances to add up over time and create a large disturbance.

Precipitation - Precipitation is rain, snow, sleet, or hail — any kind of weather condition where something's falling from the sky. Precipitation has to do with things falling down, and not just from the sky. It's also what happens in chemical reactions when a solid settles to the bottom of a solution.

Quanta - Quantum is the Latin word for amount and, in modern understanding, means the smallest possible discrete unit of any physical property, such as energy or matter.

Renewable energy - is the energy that is collected from renewable resources, which are naturally replenished on a human timescale, such as sunlight, wind, rain, tides, waves, and geothermal heat.

Reproduction - It is a biological process by which an organism reproduces an offspring that is biologically similar to the organism.

Smog - Smog is a kind of air pollution, originally named for the mixture of smoke and fog in the air.

Solar thermal power - are electricity generation plants that utilize energy from the Sun to heat a fluid to a high temperature. This fluid then transfers its heat to water, which then becomes superheated steam. This steam is then used to turn turbines in a power plant, and this mechanical energy is converted into electricity by a generator.

Super pollutants - are non-carbon dioxide greenhouse emissions responsible for an increasing share of global warming

REFERENCES

BOOKS:

Climate Change by Gillard, Arthur

Climate Change by Woodward, John

Overheated: The Human Cost of Climate Change by Gusman, Andrew T

It's Getting Hot in Here: The Past, Present, and the Future of Climate Change by Heos, Bridget

A Warmer World: From Polar Bears to Butterflies, How Climate Change Affects Wildlife by Arnold, Caroline

Climate of Hope: How Cities, Business, and Citizens Can Save the Planet by Bloomberg, Michael

Unstoppable: Harnessing Science to Change the World by Bill Nye

Natural Disaster by Watts, Claire

Atmosphere of Hope: Searching For Solutions to Climate Crisis by Flannery, Tim F.

Extreme Weather: Surviving Tornadoes, Sand Storms, Blizzards, Hurricanes and More by Kostigen, Thomas

The Polar Bear Scientist by Lourie, Peter

Global Warming by Simon, Seymour

How We Know What We Know About Our Changing Climate: Scientists and Kids Explore Global Warming by Cherry, Lynne

Is Our Climate Changing by Rooney, Anne

Renewable Energy by Langwith, Jacqueline

Renewable Energy: Discover the Fuel of the Future by Sneideman, Joshua

Why Should I Bother About the Planet by Meredith, Susan

What Is Climate Change? by Gail Herman

Get Down To Earth! What You Can Do to Stop Global Warming by Laurie David and Cambria Gordon

INTERNET REFERENCES:

https://climate.nasa.gov/

https://climatekids.nasa.gov/

https://www.sciencealert.com/

https://www.britannica.com/

https://www.ncdc.noaa.gov/

https://www.noaa.gov/climate

http://berkeleyearth.org/

https://weather.com/

https://www.cdc.gov/

https://www.who.int/

https://www.nrel.gov/

https://www.livescience.com/

http://climate.org/

https://www.nationalgeographic.org/

https://www.eesi.org/

https://climatechange.chicago.gov/

http://www.environmentreports.com/foodmatters/

https://www.c2es.org/

https://www.popularmechanics.com/

https://www.scientificamerican.com/

https://www.erc-co.org/

https://eartheasy.com/

https://www.nwf.org/

https://wwf.panda.org/

https://www.sciencedirect.com/

https://www.nrdc.org/

https://nsidc.org/

https://www.globalchange.gov/

https://www.un.org/en/

https://earthobservatory.nasa.gov/

https://www.natgeokids.com/uk/

https://iswitch.com.sg/

https://www.conserve-energy-future.com/

https://www.epa.gov/

https://www.energy.gov/science-innovation/climate-change

https://www.climateworks.org/

https://www.shipleyenergy.com/

https://savethewater.org/

https://www.wired.co.uk/

https://www.earthday.org/

https://www.hcn.org/

https://blogs.ei.columbia.edu/

https://www.ovoenergy.com/

https://www.sciencedaily.com/

https://www.lovemoney.com/

https://www.ccacoalition.org/en/initiatives/oil-gas

https://www.who.int/news-room/feature-stories/detail/climate-change-and-its-impact-on-health-on-small-island-developing-states

https://royalsociety.org/topics-policy/projects/climate-change-evidence-causes/basics-of-climate-change/

https://www.bbc.com/news/science-environment-49817804

https://www.kpbs.org/news/2020/aug/14/california-wildfires-burn-amid-high-risk-brutal-bl/

https://www.climatehotmap.org/global-warming-locations/republic-of-kiribati.html

https://extranet.who.int/goarn/content/bahamas-health-officials-respond-hurricane-dorianpaho%E2%80%99s-support

https://earthobservatory.nasa.gov/images/91291/the-ups-and-downs-of-lake-chad

https://www.nature.com/articles/s41598-017-04134-5/figures/2

https://scied.ucar.edu/carbon-cycle

http://www.global-greenhouse-warming.com/global-carbon-cycle.html

https://www.climatecentral.org/gallery/download/emissions-sources-2020

https://www.americanprogress.org/issues/green/reports/2013/06/13/66262/super-pollutants-101/

https://www.pgecurrents.com/2014/10/29/stop-vampire-appliances-from-taking-a-bite-out-of-your-budget/

https://www.energystar.gov/sites/default/files/tools/ENERGY%20STAR%20Appliances%20Brochure_508.pdf

https://blog.ucsusa.org/rachael-nealer/gasoline-vs-electric-global-warming-emissions-953

https://www.nrdc.org/resources/wasted-how-america-losing-40-percent-its-food-farm-fork-landfill

https://www.biocycle.net/wp-content/uploads/2013/08/36a.jpg

https://www.watershedcouncil.org/rain-barrels.html

https://populationmatters.org/the-facts/climate-change

https://populationmatters.org/the-facts/resources-consumption

https://www.cdc.gov/nceh/drought/

https://www.americanrivers.org/threats-solutions/clean-water/impacts-rivers/

http://priceofoil.org/2016/08/15/louisiana-floods-a-classic-signal-of-climate-change/

https://earth.esa.int/web/earth-watching/historical-views/content/-/article/global-deforestation-2012

https://www.nationalgeographic.org/encyclopedia/smog/

https://insideclimatenews.org/news/20112017/kiribati-climate-change-refugees-migration-pacific-islands-sea-level-rise-coconuts-tourism

https://climate.nasa.gov/vital-signs/carbon-dioxide/

https://climate.nasa.gov/vital-signs/global-temperature/

https://www.worldwildlife.org/stories/giant-panda-no-longer-endangered

https://medialibrary.climatecentral.org/resources/more-mosquito-days

https://www.dailymail.co.uk/sciencetech/article-6618663/10-year-challenge-face-planet-changed-decade.html

https://medialibrary.climatecentral.org/resources/2020-days-above-thresholds

https://www.climatecentral.org/gallery/graphics/2020-ticks#modal

https://ccimgs-2020.s3.amazonaws.com/2020GlobalTempCheckup/2020GlobalTempCheckup_HorseRace_en_title_lg.jpg

https://www.climatecentral.org/gallery/graphics/2020-ocean-heatwaves

https://www.esrl.noaa.gov/gmd/ccgg/trends/global.html

https://www.who.int/globalchange/summary/en/index5.html

https://www.cdc.gov/air/particulate_matter.html

https://www.brooklynbridgeforest.com/

https://whc.unesco.org/en/documents/179011

https://www.nrdc.org/stories/renewable-energy-clean-facts#sec-types

https://sites.google.com/a/ihsph.org/science-lower-school/home/team-2/alt2

https://phys.org/news/2015-02-electricity-biomass-carbon-capture-western.html

https://newfrontierdata.com/our-advisors/about-dr-joseph-romm/

https://www.nobelprize.org/prizes/chemistry/1903/arrhenius/biographical/

https://sandiegohistory.org/archives/biographysubject/revelle/

https://www.nature.com/articles/437331a

Carbon Block Puzzle

CPSIA information can be obtained
at www.ICGtesting.com
Printed in the USA
LVHW082121200321
682008LV00024B/387